C000070368

The Healing POWER of Kindness

TWENTY-THIRD PUBLICATIONS
185 WILLOW STREET • PO BOX 180 • MYSTIC, CT 06355
TEL: 1-800-321-0411 • FAX: 1-800-572-0788
E-MAIL: ttpubs@aol.com • www.twentythirdpublications.com

NOVALIS

The Scripture passages conatained herein are from the *New Revised Standard Version of the Bible*, copyright ©1989, by the Division of Christian Education of the National Council of Churches in the U.S.A. All rights reserved.

Twenty-Third Publications
A Division of Bayard
185 Willow Street
P.O. Box 180
Mystic, CT 06355
(860) 536-2611 or (800) 321-0411
www.twentythirdpublications.com
ISBN:1-58595-262-1

Published in Canada by
Novalis
49 Front Street East, 2nd Floor
Toronto, Ontario, Canada
M5E 1B3
Phone: 1-800-387-7164 or (416) 363-3303
Fax: 1-800-204-4140 or (416) 363-9409
Email: novalis@interlog.com
ISBN: 2-89507-413-5

Copyright ©2003 Jean Maalouf. All rights reserved. No part of this publication may be reproduced in any manner without prior written permission of the publisher. Write to the Permissions Editor.

Library of Congress Catalog Card Number: 2003104598
Printed in the U.S.A.

Contents

One kind thought, one kind word, one kind deed, one at a time, and the world will be transformed.

Every thought pondered, every word uttered, and every deed performed counts. Nothing is lost. Good or bad, nothing dissipates in the void. Rather, everything is recorded in the human brain and heart, in the cosmic development, and into eternity.

Violence invades our lives because we choose to keep greed, selfishness, and anger alive in our hearts and souls. If we enjoy peace, happiness, and abundance, this is because we foster goodwill, forgiveness, and kindness.

People all over the world are hungry for peace of mind, for finding solutions to their problems, for finding ways to improve their relationships with others, and for finding meaningful ways of life. A loving and generous kindness can certainly make a difference. Kindness, a precious God-given gift to us, is one of the sweet expressions of love.

Giving, not because we have to, but for the sheer sake of giving, just out of love, is something really beautiful—out of this world! This kind of gratuitous goodness—a lavish kindness—makes our world a better place in which to live, and makes us better people.

Everyone benefits from kindness. We are so deeply touched by it that we are transformed. In the holy of holies of our being, we feel connected, centered, involved, engaged, and deeply bonded to others, regardless of our divisions due to ideology, religion, race, gender, ethnicity, nationality, economic status, or other factors. After all, we are all made of flesh, bones, and blood. We belong to one human family. We all have the same basic needs. We are one. We are whole. We are human together. We are in the same boat of destiny.

We cannot be but kind together and to each other. This is written in our very nature and clearly stated in our Scripture. "You shall love the Lord your God with all your heart, and with all your soul, and with all your strength, and with all your mind; and your neighbor as yourself" (Lk 10:27). Love is the foundation of our very survival.

Kindness means empathy, true intimacy, encouragement, admiration, service, understanding, genuineness, concern, truth, trust, and all that makes us true images of God. The earnest desire to conform ourselves to the image of God and to Jesus Christ will make bitterness, cunningness, and lies disappear. The very attempt to be like Jesus and to see Jesus in every person we meet is already a source of sweetness that flows from our very being to all those who come our way. Mother Teresa of Calcutta said: "Be the living expression of God's kindness—kindness in your face, kindness in your eyes, kindness in your smile, kindness in your warm greeting." Fulton J. Sheen insisted: "There are three rules of dealing with those who come to us: 1) kindness, 2) kindness, 3) kindness."

Kindness is more important than knowledge. Kindness can reach the deepest call of the heart and soul, and lead to a different kind of world and self, while knowledge, important as it is, stops short of going all the way. Knowledge can achieve much, but kindness can *be* much.

We have certainly reached an advanced level of scientific and material progress, but our internal progress remains inadequate. A spiritual revival is a must.

I hope that this little book, with its concepts, implications, and applications, will help us better understand the reasons why we do what we do and question the adequacy of some of our lifestyles and behaviors. Being so interconnected with one another, we have the capacity to change the world simply by changing ourselves. We can make things happen if we choose. We can transform our world and our common destiny as we wish.

Kindness holds the key to the secret of our own transformation and, in the process, of the transformation of the world.

CHAPTER ONE

Kind Thoughts

Do not be conformed to this world, but be transformed by the renewing of your minds, so that you may discern what is the will of God—what is good and acceptable and perfect.

■ ROMANS 12:2

Many of us may have experienced a new heart in God. Yet we still seem, more often than not, adamantly attached to our old minds, and this is what must change.

The apostle Paul, noticing the temptations of our fallen nature and the attractions of the world, insisted in his letters

5

on the necessity of "the renewing of [our] minds" (Rom 12:2), of having "the mind of Christ" (1 Cor 2:16), of "[clothing ourselves] with compassion, kindness, humility, meekness, and patience" (Col 3:12), and on the necessity "to be renewed in the spirit of [our] minds, and to clothe [ourselves] with the new self, created according to the likeness of God in true righteousness and holiness" (Eph 4:23–24). He appealed to this transformation "by the meekness and gentleness of Christ" (2 Cor 10:1).

Although this transformation into a life of Christlike humility and kindness seems to be a daily challenge for all of us, such a change is of critical importance because our very salvation as well as our own survival on earth is at stake. Collectively, we, as human beings, need to take stock of what we think and, therefore, what we create. Do we want to participate in the goodness and kindness of God on earth or do we want evil and more destruction to rule our lives?

We Are What We Think We Are

Thoughts have the ability to shape reality. Indeed we are what we think we are, and we will be and do what we think we can be and do. If we think defeat we will create the conditions that lead to defeat. If we think success and really believe it, we will do things that lead to success.

Thoughts have the ability to shape reality.

When we surround ourselves with a negative climate of complaints and expectations of the worst, we fill our computer-brain with suggestions that will materialize in illness, accident, and depression. When we feed our computer-brain with encouragement, beautiful images, positive input, and high ideals, we will be rewarded with a positive output of good health, happiness, and general wellness.

Our way of thinking determines who we are and how we act, and affects the way others react to us. This is why a change in our thinking can change not only our own life but the life of the world around us as well.

When Albert Einstein said, "The unleashed power of the atom has changed everything save our modes of thinking and we thus drift toward unparalleled catastrophe," he was expressing his concern about the power of the mind; it can create either more beauty or more destruction on earth.

In 1989, the United Nations Educational, Scientific and Cultural Organization (UNESCO) concluded in a statement: "As war begins in the mind of men, so peace also begins in our minds. The same species that invented war is capable of inventing peace." Our thoughts release unbelievable power in this world. Thinking evil produces evil; thinking goodness and kindness creates goodness and kindness.

Most of us are aware of recent studies that demonstrate the intimate link between the mind and body. The new physics has validated the power of the mind in inventing our reality, and new medicine has proved time and again that illness and recovery are often the product of simultaneous physical, psychological, and spiritual conditions.

If it is true that the world usually mirrors our state of mind, it is also true that we feed our brain with this very world. Indeed, we feed our brain with the physical nutrients of the food we eat, the air we breathe, and the water we drink.

We also feed our brain with ideas—good or bad—found in the books we read, the television programs we watch, the movies we see, and the experiences we acquire through contacts with other people and through the different circumstances of our life. The mind food is our entire environment—all that influences our conscious and subconscious thoughts, and all that determines our habits, attitudes, and personality.

There is an inevitable exchange between the mind and the world. The world contributes in feeding our mind, and our mind contributes in creating the world in our image.

Have you ever thought about what kind of person you would be had you been born in a different religion, different culture, or different way of life? Have you thought about your present belief system, values, convictions, and how they made you the way you are? Have you thought about the way you run your life and why you behave the way you do? Have you thought about your obligation for leaving your own impact on the world, the one that gave you so much? Can you consider kindness as your gift to this world, and by doing so, be kind to yourself?

Because of the integration of our body-mind-soul, and because our psyche and soma are closely related, our thoughts are certainly powerful factors in generating our transformation and wellness. We spend a good part of our lives searching for something that makes us happy, while what we are looking for is within our very vision.

The problem is not in the "problem" but in how we see it. With a change in vision, a kind thought, and a genuine quest for goodness, a new world will unfold before our very eyes. Thoughts and intentions command the flow of our energy. When we work with our inner world, our outside world changes. Think kindness, and kindness will be.

The Power of Kind Thoughts

Thoughts are power. They are the source that gives life to words and deeds. Words and deeds remain in darkness if they are not animated by kind and loving thoughts that radiate God's light and goodness in the world.

When the prodigal son of the gospel (Lk 15:11–32) took his share of property and left to go to a distant country, his father kept thinking of him with kindness. In addition to the misery he found himself in, this son must have felt his father's kindness even from far away. Kind thoughts transcend space and time. They contributed greatly in making this son "[come] to himself," thinking, and conclude that he would "'get up and go to my father'....While he was still far off, his father saw him and was filled with compassion; he ran and put his arms around him and kissed him," before even letting

> Kind thoughts transcend space and time.

him finish his over-rehearsed speech of conversion.

It was the thoughtful kindness of the father that freed the son from the attitudes, philosophy of life, and ways of thinking locked in sin. And this same thoughtful kindness freed the older son from his jealousy, anger, and resentment, as well as from his so-called righteousness and loyalty. Both sons had a certain patterns of thought that needed to be transformed and renewed. The kindness of the father did the job.

No matter where people are in life, kindness makes them celebrate together. Kindness has something of God's benevolence.

The poor widow of the gospel, who contributed what was worth a penny to the treasury because she could not afford more, had, said Jesus, "put in more than all those who are contributing to the treasury. For all of them have contributed out of their abundance; but she out of her poverty has put everything she had, all she had to live on" (Mk 12:41–44).

Love is the key. Love gives beauty, life, and worth to words and deeds. If they are not animated by love, our words and deeds—whatever they may be—are dead. St. John put it boldly this way: "Whoever does not love abides in death" (1 Jn 3:14). The hearth does not mean much without a fire in it. A kind thought is the fire that animates the hearth. Loving-kindness is the fire. The inside "thought" is what matters. Jesus said it: "You have heard that it was said, 'You shall not commit adultery.' But I say to you that everyone who looks at a women with lust has already committed adultery with her in his heart" (Mt 5:27–28).

People often think that what is important is to conform their deeds to the law. We know now that any outward deed is the result of an inward thought. We know that any conduct we choose originates in the thoughts we entertain in our minds. This means that if we entertain a covetous thought for our neighbor's money, we are already a thief at heart, and sooner or later the outer act will materialize. If we entertain healthy, positive, and kind thoughts, these thoughts will be translated into action. Kindness begets kindness and accomplishes what rigidity and toughness cannot accomplish. When we really believe this, it will happen. Jesus promised it when he said, "All things can be done for the one who believes" (Mk 9:23).

St. Paul made clear that if we want to live Christ's life, every aspect of our minds needs to be renewed. We should allow the Holy Spirit to work with our spirit (see Rom 8:16), so that we can be transformed by the renewal of our minds (see Rom 12:2), putting off our old ways of thinking (see Eph 4:22), and putting on a new self (see Eph 4:24) resembling the "mind of Christ" (1 Cor 2:16) with his "meekness and gentleness" (2 Cor 10:1).

Do we really believe that our old ways of life, including our old ways of thinking, were crucified on the cross with Jesus, and that our new life is resurrected with the resurrected Christ? Aren't we convinced that we should put the "new wine" into "fresh wineskins" (Mt 9:17), as Jesus suggested? Aren't we convinced that our weak old ways of thinking should be replaced with the new ways of the Holy Spirit who will inspire us with new thoughts and desires, helping us to develop new perspectives?

The blessing of this radical conversion will animate all our thoughts, motivations, and decisions, and we will become a whole new creation in the Lord. Then we can be the instruments of his benevolence and kindness to our families, our neighbors, our friends, and even our enemies.

What Do Kind Thoughts Really Do?

1. *Kind thoughts enhance spiritual life.* They allow God to penetrate and dwell in the creature that we are. They prepare the way to prayer and meditation.

They align our view to God's view, which is not only the truest view, but the only true view at all. Thus, any kind of discrimination, prejudice, suspicion, bitterness, and hostility becomes foreign to a healthy behavior, and tends to dissipate.

If every day, in our morning and evening prayers, we try to foster in our heart a readiness to forgive and forget any offense we are victims of, and couple this with understanding and acceptance, we would find ourselves helping others and ourselves become better people. This is what kindness does. It transforms us by making us better people.

But to be able to do so is not an easy task, especially in a society such as ours that rewards aggression. Aggressors often think that kindness is weakness or just a sentimental feeling. On the contrary, a genuine Christian thinks that kindness is not weakness, but strength. The weak person, by surrendering to the oppressor out of intimidation, ends up in frustration, anger, and self-hatred. A kind Christian does not harbor frustration, anger, and self-hatred. A kind Christian is a challenging person—a spiritual athlete.

To be a Christian today is to be prepared to challenge indifference and aggression with love, kindness, patience, and peace, because these virtues come from knowing that one is loved by God, chosen to live by the grace of the Holy Spirit, and called to set an example for, and help transform, those who live with lesser values and ideals.

Paul wrote: "Love is patient; love is kind; love is not envious or boastful or arrogant or rude. It does not insist on its own way; it is not irritable or resentful; it does not rejoice in wrongdoing, but rejoices in the truth. It bears all things, believes all things, hopes all things, endures all things" (1 Cor 13:4–7). Without the strength of a genuine spiritual life, it would be hard to live up to Paul's striking words.

> To be a Christian today is to challenge indifference and aggression with love and kindness.

Kind thoughts, to be true, must be connected to a divine ideal where strength comes from. Only then are they understood and become effective and easier to live for, as Paul reminds us, "I can do all things through him who strengthens me" (Phil 4:13).

2. *Kind thoughts foster peace.* War starts not when weapons clash at each other, but when minds and hearts are not at peace. When we are not in harmony with God, the real and only source of peace, we are

not at peace with ourselves, nor with others. When we reconcile ourselves with God, we will start to have the kind thoughts that will effect kind words and kind deeds. Then peace takes shape.

Our religion helps us to be joyful and to share our joy with others.

If we really have kind thoughts, we naturally and spontaneously disregard the offenses that irritate our egos, turn a deaf ear to an unjust and unjustified remark, avoid starting an argument, and try not to monopolize the conversation. We will also refuse to hear a person speaking unkindly of another person and will not participate in any gossiping. Mother Teresa of Calcutta used to recommend to her Sisters, "Be kind and merciful. Let no one ever come to you without leaving better and happier. Be the living expression of God's kindness—kindness in your face, kindness in your eyes, kindness in your smile, kindness in your warm greeting."

3. *Kind thoughts bring deep joy to the heart.* People crave joy, and they don't have it. They cannot find it because they are looking for it where it does not exist. Neither amusements nor even splendid deeds can by themselves bring the joy that satisfies the thirst of our souls.

A simple kind and loving thought can do it, however. This simple kind and loving thought possesses the ability to dissipate the clouds of sadness, dissatisfaction, and depression. Kind thoughts make miracles.

Somehow when we are in the presence of people who usually live by kind thoughts, we ourselves become different. We cannot fail to notice that the beauty of their thoughts shows through their face, eyes, and the tone of their voices. They vibrate light, gladness, and goodness. They radiate joy. Nothing seems to alter this blessed state because they seem to have, almost at all times, the perfect joy that Jesus had, even the night before his death, when he said, "I have said these things to you so that my joy may be in you, and that your joy may be complete" (Jn 15:11).

Our religion, a true religion of joy, helps us to be joyful ourselves and to share our joy with others. It does not take much to bring joy to another's heart. All it takes, very often, is a kind thought that is translated in a loving presence, a cheering word, a sincere smile, a meaningful little gift, and a genuine and holy hug. These kinds of subtle loving gestures, springing from God's love, bring what "no one has heard, no ear has perceived, no eye has seen" (Is 64:4), the kindness that transforms the world.

4. *Kind thoughts make us considerate of others.* The talents and gifts that God has given us are not for us alone. They are also for all others. Our vocation—the special calling through our talents—must be oriented toward benefiting others. When we think well about others, when we wish them the best, and when we help them to be the best they can be, we cooperate in God's work in the world. When they bloom, we bloom, and the entire world blooms.

It is true that we cannot carry out all the tasks we want to do. But we can send loving thoughts to others, we can be concerned with their concerns, and especially we can pray for them. We can love them—love all that binds us to them, and that brings peace to our hearts and to their hearts.

For your Reflection & Response

1. Find a quiet, relaxing place, and give yourself about twenty minutes for meditative time. Be alone with God. Enjoy this intimate moment with the Lord. Pray for yourself, for your family, for others. Forgive any resentment you may have had far in the past or you may have now.

Try to think as you think Jesus might have thought in that particular situation. Surrender yourself and your world to him and allow him to be your companion while you are going through your own circumstances of life. You will find yourself ready to "have the mind of Christ" (1 Cor 2:16) when similar situations arise again.

2. Visualize a picture of wholeness and kindness for yourself. Visualize this same picture extended to your world, then to the world at large. Notice the flow of energy reaching others. Repeat this exercise several times.

3. Do you feel "stuck" in some area of your life? Are you stuck in a job you don't like, a location you didn't choose, a certain lifestyle you think you cannot change, a situation you don't desire, a condition that you think has no alternative?

Use the power of your mind to create what you really want by providing you with the skills you need to "revolutionize" your life as well as your world. Pick a dream, and go for it. See it happen. Dreams change the world.

4. Write on a piece of paper the following affirmation (or one similar that fits your case): "My kind thoughts transform my world." Repeat it often. Post it on your refrigerator. Sing it. Share it with a friend. In your mind and heart, imagine a picture of the end result of this affirmation, for yourself and for others. Be that transformed person you want to see in others. Create your own reality mindfully, consciously, and deliberately. Others will certainly grasp your essence and follow your steps.

5. Name one person or more that you don't particularly like and think kindly of them today, tomorrow, the day after, and always.

Repeat this phrase several times a day.

I think kindness.

PRAYER

Dear Lord, help my mind and heart to think only healthy, happy, and holy thoughts for myself and others. Without you, I know how convenient it is to indulge in petty and negative thoughts.

Help me to forgive others and help others to forgive me. Without you, I know how difficult it is to forgive "seventy-seven times" (Mt 18:22), as you recommend.

Help me to be kind. Without you, I know how easy it is to project my hurt and resentment on others. And grant me the grace to allow you to think in me, at any moment and in any situation of my life. Amen.

CHAPTER TWO

Kind Words

Pleasant words are like a honey-comb, sweetness to the soul and health to the body.

■ PROVERBS 16:24

Thoughts and words go hand in hand. Words provide a system of symbols and rules that facilitates our thinking. No psychologist can directly observe thinking, so it must be examined from the words spoken, the actions taken, and the life lived.

Needless to say, thoughts and words are so intimately connected that, as some analysts suggest, they are one and the

22

same. Our words embody our thoughts, define our being, determine the quality of our everyday lives, and allow us to communicate with one another.

Words contribute to the wholeness of life and to its meaning. They can deceive or they can build. They carry feelings and move us toward an intended direction to fulfill certain purposes. This is why we should be careful in determining our audience. An audience is not composed of everyone. The same words mean different things to different people. And if the only audience is yourself, be aware of what you tell yourself and what you feed your brain.

In any case, there is something permanent about the words we use. When we sow seeds and walk away from them, nature takes over, allowing its own being to evolve. So too the words we sow are in our being and in others. The words we speak or think are like the seeds; once planted, sooner or later, they will appear.

Words have the capacity to refer us to the sacred. Their importance for religions seems crucial. In Christianity, for example, John begins his gospel by saying: "In the beginning was the Word, and the Word was with God, and the Word was God" (Jn 1:1), equating Christ and *logos*. In Islam, it is taught that the Koran is the literal word of God.

Words, carry great potential for good or evil.

We cannot exist without words as we cannot exist without air. Words fill our lives through speech, reading, writing, and listening. Words, which constitute a significant part of our life, carry great potential for good or evil and underline our responsibility. Jesus advised us on this matter by saying: "It is not what goes into the mouth that defiles a person, but it is what comes out of the mouth that defiles" (Mt 15:11). "I tell you, on the day of judgment you will have to give an account for every careless word you utter; for by your words you will be justified, and by your words you will be condemned" (Mt 12:36–37).

Our tongue is powerful and expresses what we think: "With [the tongue] we bless the Lord and Father, and with it we curse those who are made in the likeness of God. From the same mouth come blessing and curses....Do not speak evil against one another" (Jas 3:9–10, 4:11).

How many times have we uttered words and wished we could retract them? How many times have we remained silent and later blamed ourselves for not saying what was needed? Both words and silence are important. Common sense and good judgment should help us in deciding when to speak and when to keep silent.

Words in Season

1. *"Let your word be 'Yes, Yes' or 'No, No'; anything more than this comes from the evil one"* (Mt 5:37). This means that we should dedicate ourselves to truth—say it, cultivate it, and live it. When we lie, exaggerate things, and color the truth with our own greed, self-interest, and sometimes resentment, sooner or later we make our friends or anyone who deals with us distrust us and even dislike us.

False pretense, that effort to make of oneself something one is not in order to gain recognition and to impress, is a form of lying. Hypocrisy, the act of appearing to be one thing or to believe in one thing while we are the opposite of, or very different from, what we say we are or what we believe, is one of the worst forms of lying.

Jesus was very tolerant and understanding of all kinds of sinners and the sick, but he couldn't stand the hypocrites. He attacked them boldly (see Mt 23). One is a hypocrite when one lives a double life: publicly one appears righteous but in private lives in adultery or is abusing life or has a corrupt life in business or politics. One is a hypocrite when one speaks against the very evil one practices, or when one complains of losing money while making an unjust profit.

To be bold and outspoken when truth is distorted, or when important issues of life are at stake, is not only a good thing to do, but an imperative requirement of the very truth. It is true that many things in life can be in the gray area of "both/and," but many other things must be clear and belong to the "either/or" condition. We lie to ourselves and to others when we look for ways to compromise when no compromise should be made.

Christ's words, "Let your word be 'Yes, Yes' or 'No, No,'" as well as the eighth commandment, "You shall not bear false witness against your neighbor," call clearly for the virtue of truthfulness. Our words should mirror our thoughts. Since God is truth and we are in the image of God, our speech is supposed to carry and translate that very image of God.

The first kindness we can offer to others is to be on the side of truth—to be true and to speak the truth. "Above all, my beloved," wrote James in his scriptural letter, "do not swear, either by heaven or by earth or by any other oath, but let your 'yes' be yes and your 'no' be no, so that you may not fall under condemnation" (Jas 5:12).

The first kindness we can offer others is to be on the side of truth.

2. *"Do not speak evil against one another,"* commended James. And he continued warning, "Whoever speaks evil against another or judges another, speaks evil against the law and judges the law; but if you judge the law, you are not a doer of the law but a judge. There is a lawgiver and judge who is able to save and destroy. So who, then, are you to judge your neighbor?" (Jas 4:11–12).

And do not listen to gossip and detraction either, because by listening to this kind of thing we encourage people to keep going in destroying others. Bernard of Clairvaux goes so far as to say: "It is hard to say what is worse, to injure others by words or to listen to one who does." Mother Teresa declared: "Violence of the tongue is very real—sharper than any knife, wounding and creating bitterness that only the grace of God can heal."

So, gossip is not to be underestimated, even when it is seen as harmless. In reality, it hits the very core of the person we are. It draws a wrong picture of our essence. It hurts. It leaves scars. It destroys reputations. It embodies jealousy, hatred, and at the very least an exaggerated desire to talk and talk and talk. Even if we accept our responsibility to not commit the sin of false witness against our neighbor, we keep gossiping over coffee, on the telephone, or during visits.

Mother Teresa gave her Sisters this advice: "In our work we can be attracted to idle chatter. Let us be attentive not to run this danger when we visit families. We can fall into talking about this and that, forgetting the central point of our visit. We want to and we must take the peace of Christ: let us not be vehicles of dissension. We must never consent to anybody talking to us against his neighbors."

To avoid gossip, one should try to avoid people who gossip, learn to mind one's own business, and never allow oneself to say behind another person's back what one won't say to that person's face. Thomas à Kempis, in his book, *Imitation of Christ*, had this to say: "If you will refrain from idle talk and idly running about, from listening to gossip and rumors, you will find ample time for meditation on good things."

The word of God takes sides against "a lying witness who testifies falsely, and one who sows discord in a family" (Prov 6:19), especially with slander and calumny. "Rid yourselves, therefore, of all malice, and all guile, insincerity, envy, and slander" (1 Pet 2:1), and live Christ's standard: "By this everyone will know that you are my disciples, if you have love for one another" (Jn 13:35).

Therefore, we should be very careful with our tongues. According to a Japanese proverb, "The tongue is more to be feared than the sword."

3. *"A word in season, how good it is!"* (Prov 15:23). What does a good word cost? Nothing. What is it worth? A great deal. Mother Teresa of Calcutta said: "Kind words can be short and easy to speak but their echoes are truly endless."

A good word has the power to transform lives. It is a blessing for the hearer as much as it is for the speaker. A good word carries the energy of love. It gives wings. It creates hope. It motivates action. Who would not respond to the whisper of kindness and sympathy?

There is no substitute for love. In a quarrel, a kind word often makes explanations, which usually open and reopen old wounds, unnecessary. It destroys prejudices that create enmity. A kind word consoles a lost soul and comforts a broken heart. It encourages a helpless individual and brings happiness to an afflicted one. A word of appreciation creates an instant new and friendly atmosphere. Appreciation is different from flattery, though. Appreciation is sincere and flattery is not. The first is unselfish and the second is selfish. The first works, the second may work temporarily, or not at all.

A word of appreciation encourages people. Do we really know what encouragement does? It alters lives. People feel valued. They feel appreciated, cared for, loved. They find their ways, and perhaps their purposes in life. They put on wings and fly. Encouragement can be considered as part of the apostolate of the spoken word. When we speak words of appreciation, encouragement, sympathy, the words we utter help the hearer feel better, live more fully, and be closer and closer to the Word of God.

Another form of appreciation is listening and being interested in other people. By showing genuine interest in others and talking about the things they treasure most, one can make friends more easily than by trying to get others interested in oneself. Showing true friendship is certainly one of the most refined forms of kindness.

The person who listens with love can make a big difference in the life of the speaker. Listening is a ministry in and of itself. It is one of the surest ways of reaching out to others. It can heal the speaker as well as the listener.

A good word has the power to transform lives.

4. *Keep your word*. Keeping your word is more important than you realize. By failing to make that call, to attend that meeting, to provide that help you promised, you risk making someone unhappy. And, without knowing it, you are hurting yourself. Others, little by little, give up on you. So, every time you make a promise, no matter how small or seemingly insignificant, keep your word. You show respect. People will trust you, and you become as good as your word.

5. *Watch what you say*. Words can and do hurt. It is true that aggression is usually expressed through physical assaults. More often, it is expressed by words.

Verbal expression may take several and diverse forms, including threats, ridicule, swearing, insults, or attacks on someone's character, background, appearance, or personal characteristics such as race, religion, gender, or even someone's future, such as: "You'll never amount to anything."

This kind of verbal aggression, which is common in our society, should not be taken lightly. When the victim is targeted for a long time with such behavior, the result for the victim may be shame, unjustified guilt, and a blow to self-confidence and self-esteem. But besides the victim, the attacker may suffer too, even physically. Indeed, the most common response to verbal attack is usually an attack back—if not immediately, then later on, in due time. Think about the reaction of chronically ridiculed children when they grow up. Consciously or unconsciously, they are often tempted to make their point heard, sometimes very loudly.

Words are powerful. Watch every word you say.

FOR YOUR REFLECTION & RESPONSE

1. Kind words are worth much and cost nothing. Get into the habit of saying good words. The more you speak good words, the more you will tend to change others' lives and yours in the process, and the closer you will feel to God. And the closer you are to God the more you want to practice kind things for others.

With this in mind, make a list of ten people in your home or community and ask yourself: "Do I value them enough? Do I sincerely believe how incredible they are?" Then choose someone you know who is hurting. Name three things that cause this person to feel discouraged, and perhaps even depressed. Now, what words would you say to help that person? Go and say them to that person and see what happens.

2. Do you consider yourself a good listener? Can you listen to the same story or the same joke more than once without making the speaker aware of your annoyance? Can you listen to, and understand, what others are trying to say, and let them feel how important they are? Do you really make time just to listen to your spouse and children? Do you hear all their stories? All their fears? All their troubles? All their disappointments? All their problems? All their dreams? This week, plan to listen—just listen—to someone from your circle and notice the difference it makes.

3. Do you express gratitude for any favor you receive? Is "thank you" always on your lips, ready to reach someone? Is it too difficult for you to give credit to others that would make them recognized even though the credit should have gone to you? Have you ever tried to turn the other

cheek by saying a kind word to the person who just hurt you?

4. Are you aware of the malice of gossip? Do you participate in it? Have you, by your silence or approval, failed to prevent the defamation of another person when you could have prevented it? Is the reputation of others safe when you are present or rather is it ruined because you join in the discussion of their faults and errors?

5. Do you express your joy for the joy of others? Besides Christmas and Easter cards, do you send birthday, get well, thinking of you, and just for fun cards? What three things would you say to someone who shows you an art project, or a newly written article, or a car just bought? What three things do you say to someone who cooked a meal for you, who prayed for you, or who made you laugh? Recall a time when someone helped you. Perhaps it was done in secret. How did you express your gratitude to this person?

AFFIRMATION

Repeat this phrase several times a day.

Be blessed.

PRAYER

"Let the words of my mouth and the meditations of my heart be acceptable to you, O Lord, my rock and my redeemer" (Ps 19:14).

Lord, let your Word transform me so that my words can genuinely convey your message to the people whom I encounter in my life. Let my words be kind, encouraging, uplifting, and cheerful, with the hope that all those I meet today will become, in turn, kind, encouraging, uplifting, and cheerful to others. Let your Word be in my words so that my words will incarnate in kind deeds. Amen.

CHAPTER THREE

Kind Deeds

*Whatever you do, in word or
deed, do everything in the name
of the Lord Jesus.*

■ COLOSSIANS 3:17

"Words may be deeds,"
believed Aesop. Some
masters in modern psychology,
especially the Gestalt masters,
Jean Piaget, and Maria
Montessori, talked about
thought as "internalized action."
In the words of physician and
author Leonard Laskow, "In the
subtle realms [of cellular com-
munication] intention is action."

Francis of Assisi must have
had this feeling when he said: "At

all times preach the gospel, and if necessary use words." All this echoes what Jesus affirmed: "You have heard that it was said, 'You shall not commit adultery,' But I say to you that everyone who looks at a woman with lust has already committed adultery with her in his heart" (Mt 5:27–28).

So, thoughts, words, and deeds lead, then, to each other and, before God, they must be the same.

As children of God, our thoughts, words, and deeds are various aspects of the same divine energy, for we can become, as St. Peter wrote, "participants in the divine nature" (1 Pet 1:4).

This very participation in the divine nature compels us to participate in one another's inner and outer life, because all of us have the same Father in heaven and share in a common structure of our common humanity. This foundational disposition in God and others implies the bonds of communion and responsibility that underlie our "interformation," which is our very "interbeing."

Kindness means, then, that we are in touch with both the potential and limits of our human condition. And being aware of our own vulnerability, we become able to respond easily and mercifully to the weaknesses of others.

The sacred source that binds us together allows mercy to follow, and lets us feel linked with the whole of creation in which all is interconnected and all is interdependent. But, above all, it is so, because of the Son, God's own Word of kindness, who, by entering human history and accepting the misery of the crucifixion, has transformed life into a mission of mercy and identified himself with the hungry, thirsty, sick, and outcast (see Mt 25:31–46). Consequently, the rule of the true disciple of Christ is simple and unrelenting: "Be merciful, just as your Father is merciful" (Lk 6:36).

Kindness in Action

The acts of kindness are varied and many. Here is a sample of them:

1. *Be a loving person.* Since we are made in the image of God, and "God is love" (1 Jn 4:16), every kind deed we perform must be a step toward being in the image of God, therefore loving. Deep down, love is our very essence. We cannot live without love, any more than can a fish without water or a flower without air and sunshine. Love is the most powerful energy in the world.

A kind thought about others is love. A good word spoken to others is love. But the greatest love manifests in the union of thought and word in action. St. Augustine put it this way: "We are what our works are. According as our works are good or bad, we are good or bad; for we are the trees, and our works the fruit. It is by the fruit that one judges the quality of the tree." Jesus said: "You will know them by their fruits" (Mt 7:16). And François Fenelon prayed: "Gentleness is thy work, my God, and it is the work thou has given me to do."

The fruit is the most telling thing about a being. Martin Buber underlines this truth by saying: "What is required is a deed that a man does with his whole being."

Love is the most powerful energy in the world.

Our Lord wants our life to be love in action. His commandment to us is: "You shall love the Lord your God....You shall love your neighbor as yourself" (Mt 22:37, 39), because words alone are not enough: "Not everyone who says to me, 'Lord, Lord,' will enter the kingdom of heaven, but only the one who does the will of my Father in heaven" (Mt 7:21). And he himself gave us a good example when "he went about doing good" (Acts 10:38), as Peter summarized the life of his master.

Kind deeds should be animated by a loving heart,

To keep things away from people in need is in opposition to God's will.

otherwise they remain without soul. Listen here to Paul: "If I give away all my possessions, and if I hand over my body so that I may boast, but do not have love, I gain nothing" (1 Cor 13:3). Too, the commandment of the Lord: "You shall love your neighbor," not "You shall give things to your neighbor, or entertain your neighbor, or even educate your neighbor."

So, loving-kindness is the soul of the giving, the entertaining, and the educating.

Kindness enjoys little things. If a friend shares good news, get excited about it. Listen to a concern. Celebrate a birthday. Send a card for no reason at all. Take a bunch of flowers to someone who is ill. Stop and talk with someone who has no one to talk to. Do a favor for someone without expecting anything in return. These little things not only brighten someone else's day, but they brighten yours too.

2. *Do works of mercy.* True kindness is not just a feeling of compassion or some kind of sentimentalizing empathy, but it is about doing works of mercy and relieving the pain of others. Jesus said, "For I was hungry and you gave me food, I was thirsty and you gave me some-

thing to drink, I was a stranger and you welcomed me, I was naked and you gave me clothing, I was sick and you took care of me, I was in prison and you visited me" (Mt 25:35–36).

John echoed this when he wrote: "How does God's love abide in anyone who has the world's goods and sees a brother or sister in need and yet refuses help? Little children, let us love, not in word or speech, but in truth and action" (1 Jn 3:17–18).

What we possess is not really ours. Goods are God's gifts to us. We are bound to use them and share them with others according to God's will. To keep things away from people in need is in opposition to God's will and makes it even a robbery.

Kind works of mercy are acts we perform. Indeed, feeding, clothing, sheltering, giving drink, visiting, praying, encouraging, understanding, cheering up, empathizing, sympathizing, being hospitable, burying, or giving any other form of help, though they come from the heart and go to the heart, are not only emotions but actions that involve other people. In a sense, they are political activities that transform both the receiver as well as the giver.

Acts of kindness such as altruism and volunteerism have a positive effect on health. Varied research studies have shown that by doing good deeds for others, one usually wins their affection and gratitude. The resulting warmth of this interaction is helpful in the process of self-protection from stress. Physician and philosopher Albert Schweitzer believed that happiness is found by serving others. Albert Einstein goes even further by saying that "Only a life lived for others is worth living."

Other studies have found that people who care for others are physically, emotionally, and mentally healthier and happier than those who take care of their own needs only. This is why volunteering and helping others can benefit the helpers more than the recipients of the help. Why? Because love and health go hand in hand.

University of Maryland School of Medicine researcher James Lynch wrote in his book, The Broken Heart: The Medical Consequences of Loneliness: "The mandate to 'Love your neighbor as you love yourself' is not just a moral mandate. It's a physiological mandate. Caring is biological. One thing you get from caring for others is you're not lonely. And the more connected you are to life, the healthier you are."

3. *Kindness has a cosmic scope and divine energy.* Kindness is not weakness. A weak person, by surrendering to another's will because no other alternative is possible, ends up in anger, frustration, low self-esteem, or even self-hatred.

Kindness is not mere human philanthropism either. Philanthropism that leads to the caring of one person for another and to justice-making may be an instance of kindness. But kindness goes further. Kindness is about energy we give and take from all creatures. The bottom line is the integrative interaction and the total interconnectedness between human beings, all creatures, and God. Kindness is a spirituality of solid truth, not shifting emotion; of justice, not occasional philanthropy; of genuine love, not sentimentality or masochism; of evolved adults, not fixated infants.

Kindness requires maturity, imagination, determination, and certainly a big heart. It extends to the entire universe. It is a way of being at home in the universe, with the seen and the unseen, with life and death, in God's creation and in God's presence and

More than anything else, kindness is a way of living and walking through life.

energy, which is pure love.

More than anything else, kindness is a way of life. It is a way of living and walking through life. It is a way of dealing with all that is—our selves, our bodies, our dreams and goals, our neighbors, our competitors, our enemies, our air, our earth, our animals, our space, our time, and our very consciousness. Do we treat all creation with kindness? Isn't all creation holy and divine?

4. *Kindness requires a sense of responsibility.* To be kind to our neighbor forbids certain sins that can bring spiritual harm to another person. True kindness does not allow us to cooperate in another's sin, and should not tolerate a situation where we can sin by omission or especially by scandal that encourages others directly or indirectly to follow our bad example.

Bad example, by a direct action or by omission, has an effect on others. Our Lord condemned this sin in a very forceful way when he said: "If any of you put a stumbling block before one of these little ones who believe in me, it would be better for you if a great millstone were fastened around your neck and you were drowned in the depth of the sea. Woe to the world because of stumbling blocks! Occasions for stumbling are bound to come, but woe to the one by whom the stumbling block comes!" (Mt 18:6–7).

When we are kind, we don't want to harm others, either physically or emotionally or spiritually. If our example, through thought, words, action, or omission, leads others to sin, we ourselves fall in sin, and we become responsible for the sins of others, as well as responsible for repairing the damage done.

Careful attention to others is required from us at any moment and in any situation of our lives. What we are and what we do affects others even when we are unaware of it. An encounter with another person is a responsibility. Every relationship should be a path that leads to more closeness to God.

5. *Kind deeds draw us closer to God.* Prayer, a good example, and acts of kindness have converted more sinners than eloquence, irrefutable arguments, and zeal. The woman who was taken in adultery and brought to Jesus did not need a speech on good behavior. She needed the compassionate love of Jesus' words, "Neither do I condemn you" (Jn 8:11), to turn her life around. "I desire mercy, not sacrifice. For I have come to call not the righteous but sinners" (Mt 9:13).

Sinners too are created in the image and likeness of God. They are waiting for the right word and deed to restore the beautiful image that their sins have distorted. Kindness will do it. This is a splendid service for the

Kindness is a sharing in the life of God.

converted as well as the helper. Both of them will share the same joy in God.

Kindness is a sharing in the life of God, which is the life of all holiness. Every time our selfishness is down, our kindness is up, and we grow in union with God and in holiness. John so eloquently put it this way: "No one has ever seen God; if we love one another, God lives in us, and his love is perfected in us" (1 Jn 4:12).

6. *Acts of kindness are apostolic.* Acts of goodness and altruism send a message. They testify to the reality of the Radiant One, and radiance touches others' hearts and transforms them. They reflect our true nature as children of God, children created in the image of God. This image, which is an organic living reality, is supposed to make us a living community, the way the Holy Trinity is.

Acts of kindness proclaim our nature as communitarian and interdependent. They let God manifest here and now. They testify to the value of life and humanness in all people. They demonstrate that there is more to life than just the fact of getting ahead. They inspire, show, and lead the way. They show what God is doing in the world and how we should respond.

7. *Acts of kindness enable us to live forever.* These simple things we can do for each other are, even though we may not be aware of it, real blessings. An unexpected telephone call, a warm word, a genuine smile, a listening ear, have the power to affect another person's life far more than we realize. They may heal our deepest fears of isolation and loneliness. They can make a difference in an entire way of life. They may uplift hearts and souls across generations to come.

We may never know how profoundly an act of kindness can make a difference. We live forever in what we do. Emily Dickinson wrote: "If I can stop one heart from breaking,/ I shall not live in vain;/ if I can ease one life the aching/ or cool one pain,/ or help one fainting robin/ unto his nest again,/ I shall not live in vain."

Wasn't Mother Teresa of Calcutta a living example of what kindness can be, can do, and how far it can go on in space and time? Won't her kindness live on, perhaps forever?

For Your Reflection & Response

1. Think about all the blessings you have. Think about your country, your family, your friends, your entire state of being. Look back through the years and consider the long list of kind deeds that have been done for you. Are you able to count them? Name at least five of them that have affected your life. Why were these deeds done for you and why did they affect you? Did these acts of kindness make you a better person? Did acts of kindness from unexpected individuals sow seeds of goodness in your heart and inspire you to do the same for others? Have you done that lately?

Recall a time when you felt that your life was made easier because of someone's acts of kindness. Do something special today that makes another's life easier and more meaningful.

2. *Kindness is a special form of grace.* Think about what you could have been if your parents, friends, teachers, and all the people you've met in your life had been less kind to you. And if this is not your experience, think about how the kindness of God guided you throughout your sufferings and disappointments, and helped you trans-

form these sad experiences into a source of positive attitudes that allow you to grow in kindness and prevent these same experiences from occurring to others.

We live forever in what we do.

Think about the fact that you are a child of God, that "we are from God" (1 Jn 4:6), that we should "Love one another, because love is from God; everyone who loves is born of God and knows God" (1 Jn 4:7), and because "We love because he first loved us" (1 Jn 4:19). Do you think, speak, and act as a child of God, and as others who are members of the same family?

3. Are you ready to give a hand to those who need you? What will you do if you meet someone today who seems to need a listening ear, some advice, a meal, a human connection, an encouraging word? What will you do with the pile of mail you may receive every day soliciting from you financial support for a missionary group, a hospital, a research program, a justice and peace project?

Do you realize that every act of charity toward a neighbor is an act of love of God? "Just as you did it to one of the least of these who are members of my family, you did it to me" (Mt 25:40).

A practical way to love Jesus in everyday life is by allowing him to touch others through us; by being kind, friendly, and helpful to everyone around us. Are you that type of person who sees what God sees in them? Do you see God in others?

4. When you have the opportunity, do you feel ready to use all your power to prevent evil from happening? Have you found yourself on the side of someone who suffered injustice and mistreatment? Have you ever led others, especially children, by words or bad example, to sin? Have you tried to prevent others from doing a good deed or work? Do you treat others as you would like others to treat you, by being sensitive, kind, caring, and always ready to help? Do you see yourself as part of the solution for deteriorating moral values around you? Describe your plan of action.

5. Choose three or four persons who seem irritating, aggressive, discourteous, or at least whose opinions differ from yours. Think about how Jesus loves them unconditionally, and whether you would like to love them in the same way and see Jesus in them. Consider one person at a time. Focus your attention on a specific situation.

Visualize Jesus in this situation. Think and feel what he would have thought, felt, and done. In his company and with his help, try to handle it the way he would have handled it. If you keep praying and trying, you cannot fail. Kindness transforms both the giver and the receiver.

AFFIRMATION

Repeat this phrase several times a day.

I do to others as I wish others to do to me.

PRAYER

Dear God, help me to be good and kind to others, in my thoughts, words, and deeds. Keep me from meanness, nastiness, and pettiness. Help me to get rid of my selfishness, prejudices, and pretensions.

Don't let me rush to judgments or hasty conclusions. Lead me beyond my self-centered concerns, preoccupations, and interests. Allow me to be your true disciple and witness, and your healing presence for all those who are in need. Don't let me be blind and deaf when someone cries for help.

Dear God, help me to be kind. Amen.

To live kindness seems as simple as the water we drink or the air we breathe. Air and water are so natural that we take them for granted until the moment we are struck by their absence. Likewise, kindness is mostly felt when it is missing.

Kindness is not that simple, though. It requires the ability to transcend all that separates us from others, such as age, sex, color, race, religion, personal traits, nationality, ideologies, and so on. Most of us know that this is not simple at all. It can be easy to criticize people and make them feel bad. Who cannot do that? But what takes special skills is to make people feel good in reaching their

53

Kindness, for a Christian, is strength.

potential. It takes effort, much sensitivity, and selflessness to do that.

For our society, which is run mostly by aggressive people, kindness may appear to be weakness or at best a sentimental emotion. But for a Christian, this is not so. Kindness, for a Christian, is strength. Indeed, "The meek shall inherit the land, and delight themselves in abundant prosperity" (Ps 37:11), and "Blessed are the meek, for they will inherit the earth" (Mt 5:5).

When we love one another according to Christ's commandment, we treat one another with kindness and care, and we feel the pain, grief, anguish, loneliness, and any other need of God's family members. Also we would share the joy of God's children, experiencing God's love in everyone and every creature. Kindness is love, and love is even stronger than death.

Can we, you and I, be kind in today's world? We certainly can, if we are strong enough. Do not count on being repaid in kind by a hostile society, and be ready to challenge the "values" of this society with the real values of the gospel. This is an enormously difficult task if it is not done with the inner strength that comes from knowing God's love, and from the genuineness of our own being.

Who asks the rose to bloom so beautifully and to fill the field with fragrance? The rose does this not out of weakness but out of genuineness and strength. The strength of the rose is to spread beauty without counting on being paid in kind. Kindness is like the rose in its nature and display. Kindness is what we are about. "If I...understand all mysteries and all knowledge...but do not have love, I am nothing" (1 Cor 13:2).

Kindness that is love is neither a consequence of some action nor a reward. It is God's gift to us, the gift that defines our very nature and makes us what we are. Of course we can contribute to a cause, and this is kindness too. But there is the kindness that concerns the people we meet. Persons who happen to cross our path have certain specific needs. Are we able to rejoice with those who rejoice and weep with those who weep? This is a costly business. It costs time, energy, authenticity, empathy, and the risk of vulnerability and perhaps the loss of personal safety. And so we must take care.

Kindness does not mean letting people trespass legitimate boundaries with controlling minds and malicious greed. In fact, there is more kindness in helping them to alter this kind of behavior than in just swallowing offenses. Allowing others to persist in their wrongdoing is not really kindness. Passivity can be very costly in the long run. It is true that Jesus recommended that we turn the other cheek, but it is true also that he condemned the hypocrites with the strongest terms, when necessary. He even used the whip against those who transformed the temple into a place of commerce. Kindness and truth interact beautifully.

In our nature—the capacity to think, to feel, to speak, to act—God is given to us, and loving-kindness is the mark of God's presence in us. God's infinite loving-kindness comes to us not in a sort of a wireless wave, but as the incarnated reality of our whole human experience. It is through the living of our human lives, here and now, that God continues to create us, and that we continue to enfold all our potential and truth.

Being true to God, to ourselves, and to others might be the greatest kindness of all. We were made in the image of God, and we should mirror God's loving-kindness to all creation, genuinely and without restrictions and conditions.

The superabundance of love that compels us to give, not as a matter of duty but because we cannot do otherwise, cannot empty us. Rather, it fills us up.

In giving we receive. That superabundance is the divine energy that makes "all things new" (Rev 21:5). For, in acting this way we are blessed by transforming the world, and especially by transforming ourselves.

A good thought, a word of thanks, a greeting on the street, a helping hand, and the world will be a heaven on earth.